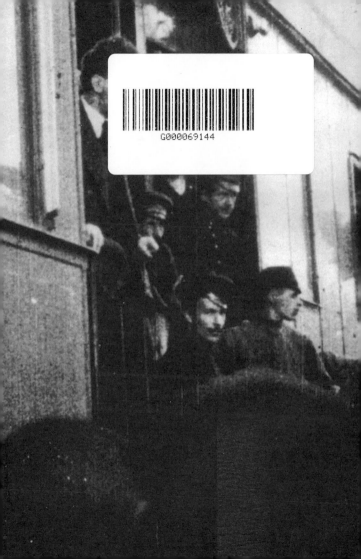

ACKNOWLEDGEMENTS

Thanks to Ian Birchall, Chris Harman, Jen Wilkinson, Chris Bambery, Charlie Kimber and all at *Socialist Worker*. Thanks are due also to many activists that I met at the Indian Social Forum in Delhi – the discussions reminded me how important Trotsky's ideas are to our new global movement. Finally, special thanks to Mark Thomas at Bookmarks for an impressive mix of patience, persistence and politics.

ABOUT THE AUTHOR

Esme Choonara is a journalist on *Socialist Worker*

COVER IMAGE
Cubo-futurist drawing of Trotsky by Yuri Annenkov

INSIDE FRONT PHOTOGRAPH
On arrival at the Finland station Petrograd, 4 May 1917, Trotsky exhorts the crowd to prepare for workers' revolution

INSIDE BACK PHOTOGRAPH
Trotsky addressing a meeting in Red Square in 1920

All images are from the David King Collection

PUBLISHED BY BOOKMARKS PUBLICATIONS 2007
10 DIGIT ISBN 1905192118
13 DIGIT ISBN 9781905192118
DESIGNED BY NOEL DOUGLAS (noel@noeldouglas.net)
PRINTED BY CAMBRIDGE PRINTING

A Rebel's Guide to

TROTSKY

ESME CHOONARA

★ 1: TROTSKY FOR THE 21st CENTURY

"A s long as I breathe, I shall fight for the future," wrote Leon Trotsky, aged 21, during his first exile to Siberia. And fight he did, through some of the most extraordinary events of the last century.

By anyone's standards, Trotsky led an amazing life. He was a key organiser of the October insurrection in Russia in 1917, and after the revolution led the Red Army against more than a dozen invading armies. He also organised in some of the darkest times — opposing the slaughter of the First World War and resisting the rise of Hitler.

Trotsky wrote at length as he debated and developed his ideas as part of constantly trying to shape the world around him. Today's world looks different in many ways to the times in which Trotsky was organising, but many of the questions faced by today's global movement against war and neoliberalism are issues that Trotsky addressed: How do you challenge capitalism in a country where most people are not industrial workers? What is the relationship between the struggle for political reforms and genuine economic equality? What does internationalism mean for our movement? How do you work with a broad range of people in a principled way while still seeking to widen the influence of revolutionary ideas?

For many today who want something better than capitalism, the idea of socialism is bound up with the horrors of Stalinism. But Trotsky was the most consistent opponent of the rise of Stalin, and the first socialist to develop a critique of Stalinism. Trotsky's unrelenting struggle against Stalin, which he ultimately paid for with his life, proved that there is a different tradition of socialism — one based on internationalism and the idea that working people have to change the world for themselves.

Trotsky railed against war and injustice all his life. In 1938 in a letter to the poet Andre Breton, he complained, "Our planet is being turned into a filthy and evil-smelling imperialist barrack" (quoted in Isaac Deutscher, *The Prophet Outcast: Trotsky 1929-1940*, London, 2003, p350). Today, as the destruction caused by war and capitalism is accelerating, Trotsky can offer vital insights to those of us trying to stop this process.

★2: TROTSKY BECOMES A REVOLUTIONARY

Trotsky "borrowed" his name from one of his jailors when he first escaped from Siberia. He was actually born Lev Davidovich Bronstein in 1879 in a small Ukrainian village. His parents were relatively well off Jewish peasants.

The Russia that Trotsky was born into was a repressive society dominated by the Tsar and the Orthodox Church. Serfdom had been abolished less than 20 years before. Most of Russia was rural and based on peasant farming, though in the towns there was a small, growing industry.

The Tsar presided over what was probably the deepest level of anti-Semitism in any country before the rise of Adolf Hitler and the Nazis in Germany. Anti-Semitism was actually encouraged by the state, which orchestrated mob violence — pogroms — against Jews. Jews were barred from settling or owning land in many parts of Russia, which is why Trotsky's family ended up in Ukraine.

Resistance to the Tsar at this time mainly took the form of a movement called the Narodniks, or "Friends of the People". They looked to the traditions of the peasant village as a way of bypassing the horrors of capitalism they saw in Western Europe. But attempts to live among the peasants and incite them to rebellion had failed, and the Narodniks had turned to increasingly conspiratorial and violent methods of resistance. In 1881 they managed to assassinate the Tsar. They hoped that this would spark a wave of resistance from the peasants, but it led only to more repression from the state.

Despite this repression, the mid-1890s saw a rising wave of resistance and defiance. In 1896 hundreds of students refused to swear allegiance to the new Tsar and 30,000 workers went on strike in the capital city of St Petersburg. This was the first strike on that scale in Russia and heralded the birth of a new force in Russia — the urban working class.

That same year the 17 year old Trotsky, now a student, joined a circle of revolutionaries based around the hut of a gardener called Franz Shvigovsky. Trotsky's father was extremely worried, as this was not what he had in mind for his son. Trotsky, a headstrong young activist, decided to stop accepting money from his family and moved into Shvigovsky's "revolutionary hut".

Like most of the workers and students he came into contact with, Trotsky at first called himself a Narodnik. People admired the bravery and commitment of the Narodniks. It was in the circle of people who met at this hut that Trotsky met his first wife, Alexandra Sokolovskaya, who already called herself a Marxist. A few months later Trotsky was calling himself a Marxist too.

Marx had argued that the growth of capitalism created a working class that had the strength to overthrow the system and a collective interest in a truly revolutionary new form of society — he called them the gravediggers of capitalism. He also famously argued that liberation couldn't happen on behalf of the exploited — that the "emancipation of the working class is the act of the working class" — a principle which stayed with Trotsky throughout his life.

Trotsky's group started agitating among workers, distributing revolutionary literature and recruiting workers to join their discussions. Surprised by their own success, they soon had over 200 members.

The police were almost as shocked by the sudden development of this small group. They arrested Trotsky along with the others in 1898. Trotsky was imprisoned for two years, using the time to read and write more widely. This is where he first read some of Lenin's writings and where he wrote what he considered his first Marxist work — a history of Freemasonry. He also agitated among his fellow prisoners including, at one point, organising an ineffectual but dramatic hat wearing protest that landed him a spell in solitary confinement.

Trotsky married Alexandra while in prison and they were exiled to Siberia, where he started writing newspaper articles and giving talks on current affairs and literature. By this time he was, above all else, a committed revolutionary and a convinced Marxist and he was getting seriously frustrated at being in exile.

★3: WHAT KIND OF PARTY?

Trotsky escaped from Siberia in a lorry of hay in 1902. Enlisting the help of other activists across Europe, he headed to London. In a house near King's Cross he joined Lenin and some of the other key Russian revolutionaries who were working on a revolutionary newspaper called *Iskra* (meaning Spark). *Iskra* was regularly smuggled to activists in Russia. Trotsky now started writing for *Iskra*.

The group working on the paper were part of the Russian Social Democratic Labour Party (RSDLP). This was a socialist party founded in 1898 at a meeting of only nine delegates, although by 1902 it had grown considerably in size and influence.

The RSDLP split at its congress the following year. Those involved were surprised when the party split over organisational details that seemed almost trivial at the time. Lenin led one side of the argument while Trotsky followed those on the other side of the split.

The argument started over the question of who should be considered a member of the party, a debate that reflected deeper divisions over what sort of party was needed. Lenin stressed the importance at this time of a tightly knit centralised organisation of revolutionaries. Trotsky thought that Lenin's model would end in what he called substitutionalism —

replacing the self-activity of the working class with a centralised party or party leadership. He supported a broader mass party on the model of some of the large parties that socialists were organising in Western Europe, in particular the Social Democratic Party (SPD) in Germany.

Lenin's concept of the party was still at an early stage of development and was shaped in part by the need to organise in illegal circumstances, facing harassment from the Tsarist police. More generally his concept was based on the idea that, while workers have to liberate themselves, they do not all have the same ideas. Some hold progressive revolutionary ideas, some hold reactionary ideas and most are somewhere in the middle. The party should group together the revolutionaries so that they can try to reach out to and influence the others.

Lenin's group won the support of the bulk of the delegates so it took the name Bolshevik, meaning majority. Trotsky went with the Mensheviks, the minority, but left them a year later. He spent the next decade trying to reunite the two groups.

Lots of people expected them to reunite, and the final formal split did not come until 1912 — and in some areas the groups didn't really split in practice until the revolutionary year of 1917. In 1903 no one could foresee the fundamentally different routes that the Bolsheviks and the Mensheviks were heading down. It would take the intense ebbs and flows of revolution, counter-revolution and war in the years between 1903 and 1917 to bring out and solidify these differences.

During those years Trotsky developed as a brilliant orator, writer and original thinker but until 1917 he didn't have an organisation to link these contributions to a wider strategy for achieving revolution. Trotsky joined Lenin's Bolshevik Party in 1917. He later said that not joining sooner was the biggest mistake of his life.

★4: 1905: THE FIRST WORKERS' COUNCILS

People sometimes imagine that revolutions are organised to schedule by a small band of revolutionaries. In reality, unexpected people or events can become the focus of years of anger and bitterness and trigger mass movements or even revolution.

In Russia in January 1905 discontent was growing with the Tsar and the disastrous war with Japan. The spark that ignited this anger was a demonstration headed by the unlikely revolutionary figure of Father Gapon. This priest and police informer led people to the Tsar to ask for reforms. The Tsar ordered his troops to fire on the demonstrators in a massacre that became known as Bloody Sunday.

This sparked a year of massive upheaval in Russia. In the next two months there were strikes across Russia involving over 1 million workers in over 120 towns. More workers went on strike in January and February of 1905 than in the previous ten years. The mass strikes triggered unrest by the peasants in the countryside, and mutinies in the army and navy including the mutiny on the battleship *Potemkin* (brilliantly captured in Sergei Eisenstein's film of the same name).

In early October a strike by railway workers became a general strike across the whole Russian Empire. When the news reached Trotsky he hurried back to Russia. He arrived in the capital on 14 October, just one day after the formation of the first soviet in Russian history, the St Petersburg Soviet of Workers' Deputies.

The soviet was a new form of organisation — a workers' council. It was the first democratic institution ever seen in Russia, with workers electing delegates to debate and vote on decisions. It was created from the immediate need to organise the strike, and at its height it involved 562 delegates from 147 factories. Its functions quickly grew from coordinating strike activity to organising the distribution of food and making decisions about arming workers against attacks by the state and right wing thugs.

The soviet united economic and political demands, inspiring slogans that encapsulated both. As Trotsky wrote, "Henceforth the war-cry 'Eight hours and a gun' shall live in the hearts of every Petersburg worker" (quoted in Tony Cliff, *Trotsky 1879-1917: Towards October*, London, 1989, p105).

The soviet started to create a new grassroots centre of power in opposition to the Tsarist state. Trotsky described it as "a workers' government in embryo". Between 40 and 50 soviets were created within three months across Russia, although none reached the power and authority of the St Petersburg Soviet.

Russia in 1905 was the first revolution to involve mass strikes, and the first to see workers' councils. In all mass revolutions since then workers have essentially organised themselves in similar ways, creating democratic forums where people can debate and organise. In Russia they were called soviets, in the Iranian Revolution of 1978-9 they were called *shoras*, and in Chile in 1972-3 they were called *cordones*.

Trotsky, more than any other revolutionary leader of his time, grasped the importance of the soviet and enthusiastically threw himself into its activities. Many Bolsheviks, in contrast, were initially suspicious of this new organisation.

At the age of 26, a young Jew in a country where anti-Semitism was rife, Trotsky was elected as a leader of the St Petersburg Soviet and became a key speaker and the editor of its news sheet.

The soviet lasted for 50 days. During that time Trotsky argued at times for the workers to advance, at times for them to retreat. He warned the soviet not to trust the Tsar's phoney promises. Trotsky drafted many of the statements of the soviet including appeals to the peasants to call on them to join the fight against the Tsar. He was involved in arming the workers against the pogroms encouraged by the state.

He later wrote of the excitement at being in the midst of these events: "Revolution appears as utter madness only to those whom it sweeps aside and overthrows. To us it was different. We were in our own element, albeit a very stormy one" (Leon Trotsky, *My Life*, London, 2004, p191).

Involvement in the soviet transformed Trotsky — he grew in confidence and ability, from a young rebel to a leader of action and ideas.

The revolution ended in December 1905 with the crushing of an armed insurrection. Trotsky was thrown back into prison. The Tsarist state had stemmed the tide of revolution for the time being, but Russia would never be the same again. Workers had glimpsed their power, demonstrated their strength and learnt to organise in new ways. The Russian working class had dramatically made its mark on history.

★5:
PERMANENT REVOLUTION

Learning from the experience of the 1905 Revolution, Trotsky developed the theory of permanent revolution — one of the most original and important contributions to Marxist ideas. It is of direct relevance to questions of revolution and liberation in the Global South today.

The 1905 Revolution created a huge debate among socialists in Russia and across the international movement. Up until 1905 many activists had been debating where the next revolution might come from and what it might be like. No one expected it to be in Russia.

Russia was economically and politically very backward compared to Western Europe. It still had a Tsarist autocracy and most people were still peasants.

It was generally agreed by socialists throughout Europe that Russia would have to follow in the footsteps of Western Europe and have a bourgeois (capitalist) revolution — like the French Revolution of 1789 — in order to build up the forces of capitalism before they could hope for a socialist revolution.

Almost without exception, all Russian Marxists agreed that any coming revolution would remove the Tsar and clear the pathway for capitalist development. The debate was what forces should lead such a revolution.

The Mensheviks argued for an alliance between workers and the liberals — who were the political representatives of the capitalist class. Lenin and the Bolsheviks argued against such an alliance — pointing to the political cowardice of liberals in practice, and arguing that the workers needed to remain independent from the capitalist class. Lenin argued that workers should fight for an alliance with the peasants to lead the revolution.

Trotsky took a new and original position. Drawing on the experience of 1905, Trotsky argued that a revolution in Russia could be a socialist revolution, led by the workers.

Marx had pointed out following the revolutions across Europe in 1848 that the capitalist class was no longer a revolutionary force. Trotsky now built on these insights arguing that in Russia it fell to the working class to be the decisive revolutionary force.

Trotsky shared Lenin's contempt for the Russian capitalists — the liberals — who had given lip service to the need for reforms, but in 1905 had proved that their fear of the workers was greater than their hatred of the Tsar. Trotsky didn't believe, however, that the Russian revolution would have to follow the same stages as Western Europe or remain within the framework of establishing a parliamentary capitalist state.

His starting point was looking at Russian development in a global context. Russia wasn't developing in the same way that France or Britain did — with small-scale artisans, then workshops, then larger factories. Driven by international military and economic competition, Russia was jumping straight to some of the most advanced industry in the world.

Trotsky later called this pattern uneven and combined development: uneven because different areas develop towards capitalism at different rates, and combined because several stages of this development can be mixed together or co-exist. You can see these patterns of development today in much of the Global South — rural peasants living by subsistence farming, or slum dwellers in shanty towns, living alongside some of the most advanced factories and technology in the world. In fact Trotsky's insights have grown in relevance since 1905 as increasing parts of the world have been traumatically and unevenly transformed by global capitalism.

Trotsky argued that, although many peasants would support the fight for change (he had after all been part of attempts to reach out to them in the 1905 Revolution), they were too dispersed and too involved in individualised production to be politically or economically at the centre of a socialist revolution.

The way capitalism was developing in Russia was creating concentrations of very powerful workers — the people who had been at the centre of the revolution in 1905. The workers were the only ones who could lead a victorious struggle against the Tsar for political freedom, but they would also find that they had to fight economic exploitation at the hands of the capitalists. This then would mean that they were in a fight for workers' power, for a socialist revolution, not just democratic reforms within the boundaries of capitalism.

Trotsky knew, of course, that workers were still a minority in Russia. The successful outcome of any revolution and the establishment of socialism would depend on the global situation — on the revolution spreading to more advanced capitalist countries. As we shall see, Trotsky stood by this internationalism all his life. It was an internationalism based on the reality of imperialism and the growing interdependence of different parts of the world — a process we now call globalisation.

Today every country in the world is dominated by capitalism, yet there are still areas where industrial workers are a minority. The theory of permanent revolution points to why even in those countries workers are the key force for change. Workers have the collective power to bring capitalism to a halt. Their struggle can give weight and organisation to the potentially explosive resistance of oppressed groups and unorganised, rural and casual workers. Trotsky's theory also points to how an effective fight for democratic reforms can spill over into a wider fight for socialism.

He never claimed this was inevitable. Permanent revolution is a theory of alternatives — the possibility exists to combine the fight for democracy and the fight for socialism, but the struggle can be captured by those who simply want to construct a bourgeois state (for a fuller discussion, see Tony Cliff's 1963 pamphlet *Deflected Permanent Revolution* available at www.marxists.org).

Democracy in Russia first arrived as workers' councils without going through a stage of capitalist parliamentary democracy. Similarly, Trotsky argued that socialist revolution was possible in Russia without going through all the stages that capitalism went through in the corner of Western Europe where it first developed. This would only be the first step — a socialist society could only be established and sustained if the revolution spread. The Russian Revolution of 1917 would bear out Trotsky's theory in both the positive and the negative.

★6: THE TEST OF WAR

The First World War, which started in July 1914, was on the surface caused by the assassination of the Austrian archduke Franz Ferdinand. In reality it was a war of capitalist rivalry and expansion and the bloodiest war yet seen in world history. At least 10 million people were killed, including 1.7 million Russians and 1.8 million Germans. It was the first war in which whole economies and therefore whole societies were shaped by the war drive.

The rulers of each nation did their best to ensure support for their war aims by creating a wave of nationalism. Europe descended into bloodshed to the sound of what Trotsky described as the "patriotic howls of capitalist jackals".

In the run up to the war all the main socialist organisations, grouped together as the Second International (the First International had been in Marx's day), had pledged their opposition to imperialist war. When war broke out, however, the majority of these same socialists fell in line with their own governments in supporting the war. The only exceptions were the Russian socialists — in particular the Bolsheviks — the Serbian socialists and a small handful of militants in the rest of Europe.

At the outbreak of war Trotsky was living in Vienna,

having escaped from exile in Siberia for a second time. The Austrian government threatened him with internment and he fled to neutral Switzerland. Here he wrote *War and the International*, a short pamphlet that was the first anti-war statement by a Russian revolutionary.

It was largely an attack on the betrayal by the German Social Democratic Party (SPD) — the largest and most established group in the Second International. Trotsky and Lenin were both shocked by the SPD's support for the war.

The SPD was a huge electoral machine, with a very large membership. It had begun to adapt to working within the boundaries of capitalism.

Some SPD members argued that they were supporting Germany in the war because Germany was a more progressive society than Tsarist Russia. Trotsky was outraged by this. He pointed out that their struggle in Russia against the Tsar was hindered, not helped, by the military intervention of another imperialist power.

Trotsky wanted to do more than oppose the war: he also wanted to understand the forces creating the drive to war. He argued that the economic forces of capitalism had outgrown the framework of the nation state. War was a permanent feature of capitalism as armed states jostled for power in an ever more integrated world market. He called for peace on the basis of self-determination for oppressed nations and an uprising of the people.

The war threw a lot of old allegiances into chaos. As well as breaking with the German SPD, which up until then he had seen as the most important party internationally, Trotsky also broke with some of his old comrades and friends who supported the war. He even wrote an "obituary for a living friend" to mark the conversion of one of his old friends into a war supporter. At same time, he also made new friends and lasting political relationships with some of those individuals in Europe who opposed the war.

During the war the differences grew between the Bolsheviks' resolutely anti-war stand and the Mensheviks' increasing wavering and concessions to nationalism. For the first time, Trotsky published some of his previous disagreements with the Mensheviks, although he was still not ready to join the Bolsheviks.

Trotsky helped organise the first attempt to pull international anti-war activists together, at a conference in Zimmerwald, Switzerland, in September 1915. There were 38 delegates there from 11 countries. Although the conference was small, it was very important, bringing together socialists from countries that were at war with each other as well as from neutral countries.

Trotsky and Lenin both agreed that in supporting the war the Second International had crossed a line and could not be reformed. From the conference at Zimmerwald came the beginnings of a new international grouping.

Trotsky was living in Paris at this time, where he was reporting on the war and helping to edit a socialist newspaper. In October 1916 he was deported to Spain. Then three months later he was deported again, this time to New York. He wrote, "I left a Europe wallowing in blood, but I left with a profound faith in a coming revolution" (Leon Trotsky, *My Life*, p260).

★7: 1917: REVOLUTION IN RUSSIA

In February 1917 a demonstration and strike of women in St Petersburg — renamed Petrograd during the war — sparked a revolution that kicked out the Tsar and brought a new provisional government dominated by liberal capitalists to power. Lenin, arriving back in Russia the following month, described it as the freest society he had ever seen — with ordinary workers and soldiers debating, discussing and organising.

The new provisional government was very unstable. The revolution had got rid of the Tsar but not solved the problems facing the mass of people in Russia — the ongoing war to which the Provisional Government remained committed, poverty, the rule of the landlords, the oppression of national minorities and the exploitation of workers by the capitalists.

Workers, learning from the revolution of 1905, had recreated the soviets as centres of organisation and debate. There existed in Russia a "dual power" — two rival centres of power — the Provisional Government and the soviets, coincidentally both operating out of the same building!

Trotsky arrived in Russia in May, to find that despite their previous disagreements he and Lenin now agreed on all the key questions facing the revolution. When Lenin had returned to Russia, he had shocked everyone by arguing in effect the same position as Trotsky — the revolution needed to push forward to socialism. Trotsky for his part could now see the importance of the Bolshevik Party in the revolution. Trotsky and his supporters worked closely with Lenin and formally joined the Bolsheviks in July 1917. Trotsky was elected almost immediately to the central committee of the Bolshevik Party with one of the highest votes of any candidate.

The soviets, as in 1905, were multi-party democratic organisations where workers and soldiers debated and organised. When Trotsky arrived back in Russia the Mensheviks and other moderates were the majority in the soviet. They had just agreed to join the Provisional Government, a move calculated by the government to increase its own credibility and make it easier to limit the demands of the revolution. Trotsky went to the soviet the day after he returned and argued against this, pointing out that it would not solve the urgent problems facing the revolution.

Lenin argued within the Bolshevik Party that they needed to "patiently explain" to the workers — to win them over to understanding why the revolution needed to be carried forward. Unhappy with the war and continued exploitation, many workers and soldiers — especially in Petrograd — had already drawn the conclusion that the revolution needed to continue to a socialist revolution, but the majority still placed their hopes in the Provisional Government. In July, Lenin and Trotsky had to try to stop a premature taking of power in Petrograd, arguing that they could take power in the capital but that the rest of the country was far behind.

This episode — known as the "July Days" — was followed by the persecution and slander of the Bolsheviks. Many of them were thrown in prison, and an arrest warrant was issued for

Lenin and two other leading Bolsheviks. Lenin went into hiding. Trotsky defiantly issued a letter demanding to know why he wasn't also on the warrant as he agreed with Lenin. A couple of weeks later he was duly arrested and the Provisional Government, supposedly a government of revolution, threw him into the same prison that he had been locked in by the Tsar after the defeat of the 1905 Revolution.

The regime continued to be unstable — many workers, peasants and soldiers were unhappy with the new regime, but so too were the right wing. In August, General Kornilov tried to organise a coup. Faced with the coup, the Bolsheviks fought to defend the very government that had put them in prison.

The Provisional Government was forced to release the Bolsheviks from jail so that they could help defend the revolution. Through the decisive role that the Bolsheviks played in defeating the coup, they proved to the masses that they were the most committed and able to defend the gains of the revolution. Kornilov was defeated without a shot being fired. Trotsky then went to the soviet and moved a motion of no confidence in the Menshevik leadership. To his surprise it was passed with a large majority. The Bolsheviks became the majority party in the soviet and Trotsky was elected president.

The choice was no longer pushing on to socialist revolution or sticking with the Provisional Government. The weakness of the regime meant that the revolution had to continue or it would face counter-revolution — the coup had proved that.

The grassroots authority of the soviets grew among people throughout this period. Factories and armed units started to ask the soviet for direction. The soviet gradually became the real decision making body in Russia.

In October 1917 Trotsky helped to organise the insurrection that finally saw the Bolsheviks lead the soviets to take power.

The revolution was almost bloodless in the capital, as the key battles for authority and the trust of the masses had already been won.

Lenin wanted the Bolshevik Party — now the majority in the soviet — to call the insurrection but Trotsky persuaded him that the party was too narrow an organisation, and that it should be called and organised by the soviets.

A military committee was set up in Petrograd — headed by Trotsky and consisting mostly of Bolsheviks, but with other left socialists and anarchists involved. Trotsky was responsible for the timing and detailed organisation of the seizure of key points of state power.

Karl Marx argued that insurrection was an art — in other words it requires some flair and imagination as well as tight organisation. Trotsky provided this flair in 1917. His role in the October Revolution was very important.

But the revolution would not have been possible without thousands of workers and soldiers, and crucially many members of the Bolshevik Party who had roots in workplaces, communities and the army, who had the politics and the organisation to fight for the revolution through the highs and lows in the struggle over many years.

★8: BEGINNINGS OF A NEW SOCIETY

The October Revolution created a new state based upon the soviets — the most democratic organs ever seen in Russia. Trotsky was asked to head the new state but he refused, so Lenin became the leader of soviet Russia.

Despite the economic poverty of Russia and the threats to very existence of the new society, the revolution ushered in some of the most libertarian and democratic measures ever seen anywhere in the world.

Workers controlled the factories and land was taken from the landlords by those who worked on it.

Trotsky was given the task of negotiating a peace treaty with Germany which, after much debate and drama, pulled Russia out of the war. Nations that had been oppressed by the Russian Empire were given the right to independence.

Trotsky often argued that the best way to "evaluate a human society is by the attitude it has towards women" (Leon Trotsky, *Women and the Family*, New York, 1973, p42). Russia had been a society where a brutal oppression of women was deeply rooted. Women were seen by many as the property of men.

The revolutionary regime transformed this situation. Women were given the vote, full citizenship, equal pay and employment rights. Revolutionary Russia was the first country in the world to legalise abortion. Homosexuality was also legalised.

The concept of illegitimate children was abolished. Either partner in a marriage could take the other's name — Trotsky took the name of his second wife, Natalia Sedova, for official documents, as did their children. Divorce was available at the request of either partner.

Trotsky understood that legal equality was just the start. The soviet state made attempts to remove the material conditions of women's oppression too — providing communal childcare, kitchens and other facilities.

The commitment to equality paid off in many spheres of life. Infant mortality, for example, dropped dramatically in the four years after the revolution, despite the economy being devastated by civil war.

The revolution transformed all areas of life including education. The number of schools doubled and the new state organised campaigns to begin to tackle the high level of illiteracy in Russia. University fees were abolished. Lenin and Trotsky both took a personal interest in the expansion of libraries. As the motivation for learning changed, so did the nature of learning itself, for example with the abolition of exams.

Trotsky was concerned with questions of culture, art and literature throughout his life. As people set about transforming their economic world through revolution, there also awoke a wider mass interest in all the questions of human existence and expression. The revolution inspired a wave of experiments in art, poetry and cinema.

Victor Serge, an anarchist who joined the Bolsheviks

during the civil war, was profoundly moved by the commitment to art he found after the revolution, even in the midst of civil war. In June 1919 as Petrograd lay under siege, Serge wrote, "I cannot help discovering in this obstinate quest for beauty, at every hour of the civil war, stoicism, strength and confidence. Doubtless it is because the Red city is suffering and fighting so that one day leisure and art shall be the property of all" (Victor Serge, *Revolution in Danger: Writings from Russia 1919-21*, London, 1997, p13).

The destruction of the Russian economy by invasion and civil war severely limited what the state was able to do, yet despite this, soviet Russia was briefly the most equal and democratic society ever seen.

★9: ARMING THE REVOLUTION

Almost immediately after the October Revolution forces began organising against the new regime. Just a month after the insurrection those loyal to the old Tsarist regime moved into action. Simultaneously some Cossacks — rich peasants — also began organising against the Bolsheviks.

Not only did the new workers' state face internal opposition, it faced invasion, interference and hostility from all the major imperialist powers. In the first half of 1918 more than a dozen capitalist armies — including those of Britain, France, America and Japan — attacked the soviet state. The very survival of the revolutionary regime was in danger.

In January 1918 Lenin officially created The Workers' and Peasants' Red Army. Two months later Trotsky was appointed Commissar for War and president of the war council. Trotsky had no practical military training or experience, although he had read military writings and worked as a journalist reporting on the Balkans War and the First World War.

Trotsky was faced with an enormous task. He had to defend a territory with a 5,000-mile border using an army that he pretty much had to build from scratch.

Even if Trotsky had wanted to use the old Tsarist army, he couldn't — it had effectively collapsed. Out of an army of about

9 million, only 40 to 50 thousand remained to defend the revolution in 1917. The soldiers no longer had the stomach for fighting, some of the old generals were now organising against the revolution, and the structure of the army was in chaos.

The masses were sick of war. One of the reasons for the success and popularity of the Bolsheviks was that they articulated the opposition to the war felt by the majority of workers and peasants. Now Trotsky recognised that if the army were to be successful it would have to have at its core people who believed in the revolution, who were fighting to defend something they deeply cared about.

When he first set out to build the Red Army, Trotsky appealed for volunteers. He built the core of the army from workers who were convinced that the revolution should be defended. Around 200,000 had volunteered by April 1918.

The number of volunteers was too small, however, to beat the huge, highly-armed forces that were attacking soviet Russia. Trotsky was forced to bring in conscription to build up the army. This brought a lot of peasants into the army and destabilised it politically and organisationally. Many peasants had a contradictory attitude towards the Bolsheviks — they were happy that they were given land taken from the old landlords, but they opposed the grain requisitioning brought in by the soviet regime to deal with food shortages in the cities.

The reality of building an army in such difficult circumstances meant that Trotsky also had to increasingly insist on strict discipline in the army. When it was first established, in a clear break with the repressive hierarchies of the old Tsarist army, soldiers in the Red Army could elect their officers. This was later abolished as more formal discipline became necessary to hold the army together and to centralise operations on several fronts. Yet Trotsky was always very firm in insisting on respect for rank and file soldiers. He rigorously opposed abuses by superior officers — both physical and verbal assaults.

Because the Red Army did not have any period of peace in which to train and develop strategy, it lacked technical skill and military experience. Controversially, Trotsky introduced officers from the old Tsarist army into the Red Army to play the role of military specialists — to be counterbalanced by political commissars who were dispatched into the army to monitor the specialists. Trotsky also called on Communists (as the Bolsheviks were now called) to join the army and to play an unofficial role in politically educating and motivating the soldiers.

Trotsky played a very hands-on role during the civil war. He wrote later that for two years he pretty much lived in a train carriage, travelling to the frontline, checking on the state of the army, speaking to the troops, developing strategy.

Several times in the civil war the revolution hung in the balance. In 1919 the "White" armies — Russians opposed to the revolutionary state — seized a town only ten miles from the capital, Petrograd. Enemy tanks appeared at the outskirts of the city. Lenin wanted to retreat from the city, but Trotsky insisted that they stay and defend Petrograd by urban guerrilla warfare if necessary. Trotsky even rode out on horseback to turn retreating soldiers round and persuade them to keep fighting, eventually scoring a decisive victory.

Against all odds, the war ended in victory for the Red Army in 1920. It was an immense accomplishment, led by Trotsky, but secured by the determination, sacrifice and courage of tens of thousands of people who fought and convinced others to fight for the revolution.

But victory came at a price. Thousands of the best communists, the most politically committed workers, had been killed in the civil war. Industry and the economy were devastated.

★ 10: SPREADING THE REVOLUTION

Trotsky argued that the world had to be understood as an integrated global system. Both he and Lenin had always maintained that the future of the revolution in Russia depended on the revolution spreading.

A mixture of economic and political upheaval caused by the First World War, combined with the inspiration of the Russian Revolution, led to upheavals across the world from 1918 to 1920. In November 1918 the German Empire collapsed and "people's commissars" formed the new government. In Hungary and Bavaria rebellion brought in shortlived soviet republics. In Italy the "Red Years" of 1919-20 saw mass workers' struggle and factory occupations. A wave of militancy swept Spain in 1918 — in Valencia strikers even renamed some streets "Lenin" and "October Revolution".

In Britain a wave of strikes and unrest broke out across the country. There were mutinies in the French and British armies. Britain also faced mass agitation in the colonies — in India and Egypt in particular, and guerrilla warfare in Ireland. There were strike waves in the US, in Australia and in Canada.

This was the context in which the Bolsheviks set up a new international organisation — the Third International or the Comintern, as it was known. At the same time as setting up the Red Army and defending the new revolutionary state from the international forces that wanted to crush it, the Bolsheviks went on the offensive by bringing together the international forces of revolution.

Trotsky played a key role in the new international from the beginning, despite being occupied with leading the Red Army at the time. He drafted the invitation to the first congress, which met in March 1919. He went on to write many of the manifestos and resolutions of the international in the first five years as well as documenting the meetings and debates.

The Comintern was based on two fundamental principles — internationalism, and the growing divide between reform and revolution.

This divide had been thrown into stark relief in 1914 when many socialist parties of the Second International had ended up supporting their own governments in the war. This is when Lenin and Trotsky first argued for a new international, based firmly on revolution and genuine internationalism.

In the growing wave of rebellion in which the Third International was formed, that clarity was needed more than ever. Many organisations that now called themselves socialist were reformists — they saw the way to get change as working within the existing framework of capitalism.

The Comintern in contrast was founded on the politics of revolutionary socialism from below — the need for workers' democracy, and rejecting the idea that you can use the capitalist state to bring about socialism.

The first congress in 1919 was fairly small and unrepresentative. The growing unrest around the world, however, meant that many organisations and individuals were becoming more radical, and increasing numbers of groups joined the Comintern. By the second congress in the summer of 1920, the Third International had become a mass organisation.

Trotsky and Lenin believed that revolution in the West — in one of the key centres of capitalism — was necessary to secure the future of the international revolution. But they both also understood the importance of the revolts by those oppressed by colonialism and imperialism.

As Trotsky put it in 1919, while on the frontline with the Red Army, "The road to Paris and London lies via the towns of Afghanistan, the Punjab and Bengal" (quoted in Isaac Deutscher, *The Prophet Armed: Trotsky 1879-1921*, London, 1954, pp456-457).

Many of those struggling against colonialism took inspiration from the Bolsheviks — from their successful revolution and from their progressive policies towards oppressed nationalities.

The Bolsheviks made specific efforts to try to reach out to oppressed people around the world. For example, in 1920 the Bolsheviks organised a Congress of the Peoples of the East, in Baku in Azerbaijan, attended by over 2,000 delegates, to bring people across Asia together to debate how to spread revolution across the East.

★11: THE UNITED FRONT

The Comintern brought revolutionaries from around the world together to debate strategy and tactics. For Trotsky and Lenin, it was a key arena to argue for spreading revolution. By the third congress in June and July 1921, it was clear that capitalism had survived the first great wave of revolutionary struggles after the war. In these circumstances, the question facing groups in the Comintern was how to build in a situation where immediate revolution was off the agenda. Trotsky called this congress "the highest school of revolutionary strategy".

The most crucial discussion at this congress, and one which has many insights to offer activists today, was a discussion on the united front. In this debate and in his writings shortly after it, Trotsky spelt out his ideas for how revolutionaries should work with others — working class people who are not revolutionaries — in a principled and united way.

The strategy of the united front flowed firstly from the genuine need workers feel for unity against the attacks and brutality of capitalism. Trotsky argued, "The working masses sense the need of unity in action, of unity in resisting the onslaught of capitalism or unity in taking the offensive against it" (Leon Trotsky, *First Five Years of the Communist International*, vol 2, London, 1974, p92).

Secondly, outside the highest points of revolutionary struggle, only a minority of workers hold revolutionary ideas. Most people for most of the time under capitalism feel that the way to improve their lives is within the framework of capitalism — they accept reformist ideas. Revolutionaries should not cut themselves off from these people.

Trotsky argued against presenting ultimatums to the movement. Insisting that people agree with everything you say before you will work with them is not a serious attempt to build unity.

This is not to say that Trotsky didn't care about winning people to revolutionary politics. His point was that ideas change in struggle, and that in the process of struggling together for common goals, revolutionaries had the possibility of showing through the real tests of struggle why revolution is the way forward.

This was how the Bolsheviks had won the masses to the revolution in 1917 when they proved that they were the best fighters against the coup by Kornilov. Trotsky argued against people who saw winning reforms as unimportant, as all small or large victories can give confidence to people.

In most countries the revolutionary groups had only recently split from reformists. Trotsky argued that they were right to split and form independent organisations, and that this independence and political clarity should be maintained. They needed to work with others in a way that acknowledged these differences but that didn't cut them off from the masses.

Trotsky also argued against ignoring reformist leaders. One of the jobs of revolutionaries was to expose these leaders as unwilling to lead serious struggle. But that couldn't be done by bypassing them or simply denouncing them — they had to be exposed in the process of struggle.

This has important lessons for trade unionists and campaigners today. Trotsky wrote that the guiding principle of the united front should be, "With the masses always; with the vacillating leaders sometimes, but only so long as they stand at the head of the masses... It is necessary to make use of vacillating leaders while the masses are pushing them ahead, without for a moment abandoning criticism of these leaders. And it is necessary to break with them at the right time when they turn from vacillation to hostile action and betrayal" (Leon Trotsky, *Writings on Britain*, vol 2, London, 1974, p141).

The theme of the united front was one that Trotsky came back to many times over the rest of his life. He discussed the question concretely in his writings about the rise of fascism in Germany and about France and Spain in the mid-1930s — where Trotsky opposed Stalin's strategy of the 'popular front' when workers' interests were subordinated to those of "liberal" capitalists.

The united front remains a key strategic tool for revolutionaries today. It provides a method both to build serious effective united campaigns — the Stop the War Coalition is the most important example of this in Britain in recent years — and to fight within those struggles to loosen the hold of reformist ideas.

★12: THE RISE OF THE BUREAUCRACY

The Bolsheviks emerged victorious from the Civil War, but Russia was in ruins. Gross industrial production in 1921 was only 31 percent of the 1913 level. It was even lower for large-scale industry. Steel production fell to only 4 percent of the 1913 output. Transport ground to a halt; there were fuel shortages, famine and disease.

The collapse of industry was accompanied by the destruction of the very working class who had made the revolution. Many workers faced the prospect of mass unemployment and had to return to the countryside to seek food.

The Bolsheviks were left running a state on behalf of a class that now barely existed, in a country racked with poverty and famine.

The Communist government under Lenin and Trotsky tried different ways to rebuild the infrastructure and economy of Russia. There were many arguments about how to do this and no one, not even Lenin or Trotsky, got their own way on every issue.

During the civil war the economy had relied on forced grain requisitioning from the peasants to feed the army and the workers in the cities. Under growing pressure from revolts in the countryside, the Bolsheviks introduced limited market reforms, known as the New Economic Policy, to provide production incentives for the peasants.

Trotsky and Lenin saw this as a temporary solution. Whatever short-term measures they took to improve the desperate situation in Russia, the real solution lay in the possibility of the revolution spreading, especially to Western Europe. This was the only way in which the pressures on the Russian economy could be overcome and the political and numerical strength of the working class be rebuilt.

In the chaos and destruction of post civil war Russia, one group began to grow in size and importance — the state bureaucracy — the administrators and officials who increasingly ran the day to day affairs of the country. These people gradually came to represent their own set of interests and to become a privileged layer above the rest of society. It was this growing bureaucracy that shaped Stalin — a second rank Bolshevik leader who came to embody the interests of this layer of society.

Trotsky and Lenin were both wary of the growing bureaucracy. As early as January 1921 Lenin warned of "bureaucratic distortions". Trotsky in 1929 described the political character of the bureaucracy: "The majority of this officialdom which has risen up over the masses is profoundly conservative... It is this conservative layer, which constitutes Stalin's most powerful support" (Leon Trotsky, *Writings 1929*, New York, 1975, p47).

Lenin became increasingly critical of the rising bureaucracy. Just before he died in 1924, he wrote what has come to be known as his "testament" in which he called for the removal of Stalin from the leadership of the party. The central committee of the Bolshevik Party decided not to make this testament public. Trotsky, wary of an open split in the party, went along with this despite sharing Lenin's criticisms.

Stalin was already deeply embedded in the bureaucracy and involved in numerous state committees by 1924. He took advantage of the death of Lenin to consolidate his own position. He stage-managed Lenin's funeral and, to the dismay of Lenin's widow Nadezhda Krupskaya, used it to put himself forward as the true heir of Lenin. From here onwards the attacks on Trotsky and the politics that he represented increased.

★13: SOCIALISM IN ONE COUNTRY

Trotsky saw the danger in the growing bureaucracy and looked for ways to stop its rise. He founded the Left Opposition which proposed planned industrialisation to increase the size and social weight of the working class, to raise its living standards and to expand workers' democracy.

Stalin and his supporters opposed these measures. Instead they maintained a slow and cautious balance between industry and agriculture, and allowed increasing market incentives in production which began to lay the ground for the restoration of capitalism.

Crucially of course, Trotsky looked to spreading the revolution as the only way to overcome Russia's poverty and to escape the pressures of international capitalism. The international movement suffered a crucial defeat, however, in Germany in 1923. The German revolutionaries lost, not because of lack of opportunity or numbers, but because their party was inexperienced, weak and divided.

Following the defeat in Germany, Trotsky wrote *Lessons of October*. Here he looked at the decisive role of a confident revolutionary party, capable of overcoming inevitable hesitations, in ensuring the success of the Russian Revolution, in contrast to what had just happened in Germany.

The publication of *Lessons of October* opened a new wave of attacks on Trotsky. Stalin and his supporters created "Trotskyism" at this time — a series of lies about what Trotsky represented — and called for war on Trotsky's influence in the party. In particular they played up the fact that Trotsky had only joined the Bolsheviks in 1917, and went on to attack Trotsky's theory of permanent revolution.

The defeat in Germany fed pessimism and passivity among the workers and peasants in Russia who were already weary from years of hardship and war.

At the end of 1924 Stalin first laid out the term "socialism in one country" in an article that he wrote attacking Trotsky's theory of permanent revolution. The idea that Russia could be a socialist country surrounded by capitalism was an enormous retreat from the vital task of spreading the revolution. It was a huge blow against the internationalism at the heart of Marxism. Trotsky had insisted that either the revolution would spread or the pressures of international capitalism would eventually destroy the revolution. Stalin's talk of building socialism in Russia alone simply evaded this dilemma.

In 1928 reality caught up with the bureaucracy. Under threat of possible war with Britain and facing a crisis in the countryside, Stalin made a panic turn to forced collectivisation in the countryside, with the state forcibly taking control of the peasants' land, and brutal rapid industrialisation in the towns. This was the very opposite of Trotsky's programme for industrialisation — far from increasing workers' democracy it involved a huge assault on workers' living standards.

This was the inevitable logic of building "socialism in one country" — Russia was compelled to attempt to catch up with the advanced capitalist countries. As Stalin explained in a speech to managers in 1931, "We are 50 or 100 years behind the advanced countries. We must make good this lag in ten years. Either we do this or they crush us" (quoted in Isaac Deutscher, *Stalin*, London 1988, p328).

Competing economically and militarily with the capitalist world had implications for the regime in Russia itself. The first of the Five Year Plans, beginning in 1929, meant a dramatic drop in living standards, and mass starvation. From 1928 to 1930 the number of people in labour camps increased 20 times over. In order to enforce this system, Stalin relied on an increasingly repressive regime and the crushing of all political opposition. All remaining vestiges of democracy were destroyed.

"Socialism in one country" also had a disastrous impact on the international Communist movement. From being an international school of strategy and tactics, the Comintern became a body increasingly shaped by the needs of Stalin's foreign policy. This meant some abrupt zigzags in strategy with terrible consequences as the interests of the working class were sacrificed time and again to the needs of the Stalinist bureaucracy.

In 1926 Trotsky joined with Zinoviev and Kamenev, former allies of Stalin, to found the United Opposition. The history of animosity between Trotsky and Zinoviev and Kamenev made it difficult for their supporters to trust each other. In order to hold this alliance together, both sides made many compromises — even to the point where Trotsky temporarily recanted his theory of permanent revolution.

With the mass of workers and poor peasants weakened from war and starvation, the opposition had a very limited base with which to challenge Stalin and the bureaucracy. The opposition was smashed. An attempt to rally support for the opposition on the tenth anniversary of the 1917 Revolution was used as an excuse to expel Trotsky from the Communist Party. Only ten years after organising the insurrection of October 1917, and only six years after helping to defeat some of the strongest imperialist armies in the world, Trotsky was expelled from his party and then exiled.

★14: THE PLANET WITHOUT A VISA

Trotsky was deported at Stalin's orders to Alma Ata in the far east of Russia in January 1928. From Alma Ata he was deported again a year later to Turkey where he settled on the island of Prinkipo.

He spent more than four years in Turkey, but not through choice. Trotsky describes this time as being on "the planet without a visa". No country wanted him on their soil — he was seen as too subversive — and so he was refused entry to all the self-proclaimed democracies of Europe.

Eventually his supporters won him short and stressful stays in France and then Norway, but when the Norwegian government banned him from openly organising against Stalin's attacks on him, he once again looked for another home.

At the end of 1936 the great artist Diego Rivera persuaded the Mexican government to grant Trotsky asylum. He lived in Mexico until he was murdered at the hands of an agent of Stalin's secret police in 1940.

Throughout this exile Trotsky wrote extensively. Many of Stalin's smears of Trotsky involved a rewriting of Trotsky's role in the Russian Revolution and his relationship with Lenin.

Trotsky wrote a series of books to set the record straight including his autobiography *My Life* and his *History of the Russian Revolution* — one of the finest examples of historical writing and one of Trotsky's greatest achievements.

Despite his isolation Trotsky followed the twists and turns of politics around the world and wrote extensively on strategy and tactics facing the movements in many countries.

Like Marx, Engels and Lenin, Trotsky believed in the unity of theory and practice. Even in exile or under guard, always with tiny forces compared to those of Stalin, he did all he could to organise his supporters internationally. Trotsky tried to organise against the disastrous role of the Comintern under Stalin and railed against the mistakes that it made. The gravest of these was the role played by the Germany Communist Party — under the guidance of the Comintern — in allowing Hitler to come to power.

★15: FIGHTING FASCISM

Trotsky called the rise of fascism in Germany the "greatest defeat in working class history". Hitler came to power in January 1933. For the three years before, Trotsky warned of the danger, arguing that the victory of fascism would be a defeat not just for the German working class but for all progressive forces across Europe.

He argued that fascism could be stopped — the organisations of the working class in Germany were bigger than anywhere else at this time. In 1932 the reformist Social Democratic Party (SPD) had over a million members and the German Communist Party (KPD) had nearly 300,000 members, and both groups had over 50,000 each in their youth organisations.

In the parliamentary elections of September 1930 the SPD and the KPD combined won more than twice as many seats as the Nazis. Even in March 1933 — after Hitler had taken power, banned the KPD and launched terror against the left — the SPD and KPD polled 12 million votes between them. But more than votes, Trotsky argued that the working class had the strength of collective organisation rooted in the factories at the heart of the German economy.

Trotsky argued that the only way Hitler and the Nazis could be stopped was through a united front between the Communists and the Social Democrats. This flew in the face of the policy of the Communist Party who strictly adhered to the perspectives and strategy coming from Stalin's Comintern.

The Comintern made a sharp turn in 1928 to what it called the Third Period. The First Period was the revolutionary upsurge of 1917 to 1923; the Second Period was seen as the capitalist stability of 1923 to 1928 — a period which, as Trotsky had pointed out, included terrible mistakes through reliance on nationalists in China and trade union bureaucrats in Britain.

The Third Period, according to Stalin and the Comintern leaders, was characterised by the final crisis of capitalism. This meant a sharp turn to a supposedly "revolutionary offensive". This involved setting up separate "red" (effectively Communist only) trade unions, rejecting the united front and seeing the social democrats — now described as "social fascists" — as the main enemy!

Trotsky in contrast argued that there was no evidence that the economic crisis was producing revolutionary mass radicalism. He called again and again for the Communists to pressurise the social democrats to enter a united front against fascism.

His based his strategy on a powerful analysis of fascism. He argued that fascism is a "counter-revolutionary movement of despair" based on the middle classes. The middle classes were driven into a frenzy of fear and insecurity by the economic crisis that hit Germany in the early 1930s. Trotsky wrote that Hitler should be seen in this context — as the living embodiment of this frenzied middle class.

The middle class may form the mass base of fascism, but Trotsky argued that Hitler could not have come to power without support from some sections of the capitalist class. Capitalists normally prefer bourgeois democracy — they only turn to fascism when they face an acute crisis. Trotsky likened this to someone who fears the dentist, but is driven to go when their toothache gets bad enough. In the economic collapse of the early 1930s German capitalists saw in Hitler a chance to destroy all working class organisation, paving the way to restoring their profits.

Trotsky argued that because this is the main function of fascism, it destroys all forms of working class organisation – even parliamentary democracy. This proved to be the case in Germany with all forms of self-organisation – even the boy scouts – being banned. This is why the SPD's strategy of constitutional opposition could not work – the Nazis had no respect for constitutional forms and destroyed every element of democracy as soon as they were able.

Trotsky also described the use of racism – the "invention of race" as he called it – used by the Nazis to weld together support for the regime.

The Communists were not strong enough on their own to defeat fascism. Yet they continued with the suicidal policy of seeing the SPD as the main enemy and seemed to go out of their way to create divisions between rank and file Communist Party members and the SPD.

Trotsky argued that the one thing that could stop fascism would be the united action of the millions of workers organised in unions and political parties in Germany at the time. He also argued that such united fronts would be a way in which to move from defensive organisation to offensive – towards soviet-type organisations. His calls fell again and again on deaf ears.

This was never going to be an easy argument in Germany. The social democratic leaders had created the conditions in which Communist leaders Rosa Luxemburg and Karl Liebknecht had been killed just over a decade earlier. But Trotsky argued it was vital to try to build unity. He was able to point to a couple of very small examples where this unity was built, crucially places where he had supporters on the ground. However, these remained small, isolated exceptions to the general picture.

For all Trotsky's brilliance, no one listened to him. He had tiny forces in Germany that never numbered more than 500 supporters. His supporters distributed a fortnightly paper for a while and then a duplicated information sheet. Many of his books and writings were available, but had no real impact.

Increasingly aware of what fascism would mean, but unable to prevent it, Trotsky warned the workers, "Should fascism come to power, it will ride over your skulls and spines like a terrific tank" ("For a Workers' United Front against Fascism", 8 December 1931, available at www.marxists.org.uk). Tragically, he was right.

★16: REVOLUTION BETRAYED

Up until 1933 Trotsky believed that the Comintern and the Russian Communist Party could be reformed. After the Communist Party in Germany — following advice from Russia — let Hitler come to power without even a fight, he no longer believed this was possible. He now thought that there needed to be a political revolution in Russia and a new International.

It was another five years before, in 1938, 21 delegates from 11 countries met in a house in France and declared themselves the Fourth International. With the limited exception of the US delegate, they represented tiny forces. Unlike the Third International, which had been launched at a time of rising mass movements and soon attracted many large groups to their banner, the Fourth International was launched in the wake of a prolonged period of defeats, the rise of fascism and the looming shadow of the Second World War. This meant that it never broke out of its isolation.

In 1936 Trotsky wrote *The Revolution Betrayed* in which he looked in detail at the reality of Stalinist Russia. This was in part a fight to reclaim the genuine meaning of socialism as a system based on equality, freedom and democracy. Stalin had just declared that Russia had achieved socialism. Trotsky argued that Stalin's Russia was not socialist — spelling out in detail the growing inequality. Looking once more at the question of women in society, he wrote, "It is unforgivable in the presence of prostitution to talk about the triumph of socialism" (Leon Trotsky, *The Revolution Betrayed*, New York, 1989, p149).

Today the crimes of Stalin are well known the world over. That was not the case in the 1930s. Trotsky was the first socialist to attempt a detailed Marxist analysis of Stalinist Russia. His criticisms were pioneering and politically explosive. Trotsky pointed out that Stalin had reversed the gains of the October Revolution. For example, Stalin recriminalised abortion, made divorce a privilege for those who could pay for it, and encouraged a return to the old forms of the family with its narrow and oppressive role for women. The commitment to genuine national liberation was replaced by the return of Russian chauvinism and the destruction of national rights.

The rise of the bureaucracy and Stalin was a new phenomenon. Although Trotsky was unrelenting in his criticism of Stalin, even he underestimated how deep the counterrevolution under Stalin had gone. He wrongly thought that Russia at this time was still some kind of workers' state. Later socialists such as Tony Cliff, the founder of the International Socialists which became the Socialist Workers Party, built on Trotsky's analysis but argued that Russia under Stalin was a state capitalist regime — a form of capitalism, shaped by international competition, run by the state itself rather than by individual firms.

In order to enforce a massive assault on the living standards of workers and peasants, Stalin went to increasing lengths to clamp down on any form of dissent or opposition. He denounced Trotsky and others who opposed the regime as terrorists and agents of fascism. Stalin deliberately whipped up panic and fear by creating myths about the threat of "Trotskyism", even resorting to using anti-Semitism to bolster opposition to Trotsky and other Jewish opponents of the regime. These fears provided a useful diversion from anger with the Stalinist regime itself.

There was a massive purge of opposition from the party. In particular there was a purge of the old Bolsheviks, including former supporters of Stalin, who had been part of the 1917 Revolution. Many were herded into camps or put on trial.

Stalin set out to break these people, demanding that they degrade and humiliate themselves in public by falsely confessing and accusing others of being agents of fascism or conspiring to plot terrorist acts. Many refused and were summarily shot. Others agreed, maybe broken by torture or despair, or politically blackmailed by the argument that failing to support Stalin was tantamount to supporting Hitler, or maybe even hoping for some reprieve.

Nothing speaks more of the despair and horror of Stalin's counter-revolution than the accounts of old Bolsheviks — brave fighters who had withstood torture, prison and hardship under the Tsar — breaking down and grovelling on Stalin's orders.

From 1935 to 1937 Stalin staged a number of show trials involving leading Bolsheviks. These included the trials of Zinoviev and Kamenev who had been on the central committee of the Bolsheviks in 1917, then allies of Stalin and then part of the United Opposition with Trotsky. They were forced to humiliate themselves publicly in heartbreaking scenes of self-abasement, by denouncing themselves and Trotsky as agents of fascism. Even this didn't save them from execution.

In fact, all remaining members of the central committee of 1917, with the exception of Stalin, Trotsky who was in exile, and Alexandra Kollontai who was now an ambassador, were executed at this time. Stalin tried to portray himself as the true heir of Lenin. Even today many people associate Lenin with the crimes of Stalin. Yet nothing illustrates more clearly the break between the October Revolution led by Lenin and Trotsky and the monstrous regime of Stalin than Stalin's need to literally wipe out the true legacy of October 1917. As Trotsky put it in 1936, "The present purge draws between Bolshevism and Stalinism not only a bloody line but a whole river of blood" (quoted in Tony Cliff, *Trotsky 1927-1940: The Darker the Night the Brighter the Star*, London, 1993, p359).

One of Stalin's agents murdered Trotsky in his home in Mexico in 1940. Stalin didn't just kill Trotsky — he destroyed his entire family. One of Trotsky's daughters died of tuberculosis after being expelled from the Communist Party and barred from working. His other daughter, Zina, was driven to suicide. Their husbands were sent to labour camps in Siberia. Trotsky's eldest son, Leon Sedov, known as Lyova — with whom Trotsky worked very closely in exile — was poisoned by Stalin's secret police in 1938. Even Trotsky's youngest son, a scientist who deliberately avoided politics, was imprisoned in 1934 and sent to Stalin's camps. He was last heard of when he went on hunger strike in 1936. Trotsky's first wife Alexandra, who was herself active in the opposition, was expelled from Leningrad in 1936 and eventually shot in 1938.

This is not just a tale of personal tragedy; it is a sign of how far Stalin would go to destroy his opponents and to destroy the legacy of the October Revolution. As Trotsky's son Lyova put it, Stalin "hates Trotsky as a living embodiment of the ideas and traditions of the October Revolution" (Leon Sedov, *The Red Book: On the Moscow Trials*, London, 1980).

★ 17: COULD TROTSKY HAVE BEATEN STALIN?

Many historians try to portray the battle between Trotsky and Stalin as the battle of two despotic strong wills fighting for power. Taken as individuals, however, Trotsky's skills far outweighed Stalin's. Unlike Trotsky, Stalin played a minor role in 1917. Sukhanov, who chronicled the revolution, recalled that "Stalin ... produced — and not only on me — the impression of a grey blur" (quoted in Tony Cliff, *Trotsky 1923-1927: Fighting the Rising Stalinist Bureaucracy*, London, 1991, p11). By contrast, Trotsky was well known among friends and enemies alike for his oratory and literary skills, and as the organiser of the 1917 insurrection and the victorious Red Army.

But the fight between Trotsky and Stalin was not a battle of individuals. They represented two different forces in Russia. Trotsky's political base was the working class — the people who had made the October Revolution. Stalin's base was in the growing bureaucracy.

By the end of the civil war the bureaucracy far outnumbered the working class. In 1921 there were around 5.9 million state officials in Russia, compared to only 1.25 million productive workers.

As industry was rebuilt after the civil war, the number of workers did go up, but they were still too weak politically and numerically, and too demoralised, to put up a fight against Stalin.

This is why, despite the huge respect that Trotsky had commanded as a leader of the revolution and then the Red Army, there was no mass rising to support him when he was witch-hunted and exiled.

Trotsky has been criticised by some, including many who support his ideas, for making tactical errors — for not immediately confronting Stalin as Lenin's last testament urged him to do, for example. It is true that he sometimes kept quiet when he could have spoken out. Sometimes he made compromises that maybe he shouldn't have. However, none of these things would have been decisive.

The fate of soviet Russia hung on the question of the revolution spreading. The international capitalist class made sure that Russia was isolated and this created the circumstances in which Stalin rose to power.

Stalin's base rested on the strength of the bureaucracy, and on the weakness and demoralisation of workers and revolutionaries. Every failure of revolution internationally further eroded workers' confidence and encouraged them to place hope in change from on high. And the stronger Stalin's position, the more he turned the Communist Parties abroad into agents of Russian foreign policy, which in turn promoted strategies that helped to secure more international defeats.

Although Trotsky was defeated, his principled opposition proves that there is a different tradition to that of Stalin. Trotsky remained true to the democratic and internationalist spirit of the October Revolution. Central to Marx's theory of revolution is the idea that working people have to change the world for themselves. This is the tradition in which Trotsky stood. If he hadn't fought, even against all odds, it would have been a tradition that could have been broken forever with the rise of Stalin.

★18: TROTSKY'S LEGACY

Two guiding principles stand out from Trotsky's life and his writings — internationalism and a profound commitment to socialism from below. Today, with mass movements around the world against war and neoliberalism, there is a growing awareness of international struggles. Trotsky supported the exploited and oppressed around the world, but he argued that internationalism should mean more than solidarity — it means seeing each struggle in the context of the world economy. Writing years before the modern theorists of "globalisation", Trotsky argued that the world had to be understood as an integrated whole — a global economy and a global struggle.

He wrote, "Internationalism is no abstract principle but a theoretical and political reflection of the character of world economy, of the world development of productive forces, and of the world scale of the class struggle" (Leon Trotsky, *The Permanent Revolution*, London, 2004, p9).

Starting with a view of the world as an integrated whole shaped all of his activity — his development of the theory of permanent revolution, his opposition to imperialist war, his commitment to spreading the revolution and his involvement in the international movement.

This perspective and Trotsky's understanding of combined and uneven development point us to some strategic conclusions for today. There are far fewer peasants in the world than when Trotsky was writing — most people who work on the land now are agricultural workers, their lives and work shaped by capitalism and big business.

But the new sprawling slum cities of the Global South are characterised by hundreds of displaced unorganised poor, living at the margins of the economy. In many cities, such as those in parts of Latin American, the poorest are the indigenous people who have faced decades of racism on top of exploitation and poverty. These groups of the indigenous and "informal" workers create an unstable and explosive element to the modern cities of the Global South. They can trigger revolts and explosive rebellions. Ultimately these struggles need to link with the power of organised workers who are strategically located at the heart of the capitalist economy. Such a combination of struggles can offer the potential for revolution.

The theory of permanent revolution also suggests ways in which the struggle for democratic rights and reforms can spill over into the struggle for economic liberation — for workers' control — and why these questions cannot be solved within individual nation states.

For the poorest countries today, there is no solution within the boundary of the nation state. The solution for the Palestinians, for example, lies in the wider struggles of workers across the Middle East — most importantly in Egypt. Socialism is impossible in one country, however rich. This is a hundred times more true for regions such as sub-Saharan Africa.

Trotsky's commitment to revolution was not just about the high point of insurrection. For him, like Marx, liberation has to be the act of working people themselves. One of the obvious problems with this is that for most of the time the majority of people don't see the need or have the confidence in their own abilities to believe that revolution is possible. From this comes Trotsky's concern with strategy and tactics for building mass movements and winning people from reformism towards revolutionary ideas.

Today we see a new generation of mass movements around the globe, accompanied by a growing erosion in the belief that the traditional social democratic parties — like New Labour in Britain — can deliver anything for working people. In this context Trotsky's strategy of the united front is a vital tool to find ways of building broad and principled campaigns. In every struggle, big or small, there is an argument between the tactics of reformism — change from above and within the limits of the state — and methods that are shaped by the approach of revolutionaries: self activity, mass involvement, struggle from below and a willingness to challenge the state. It is in these struggles that ideas can begin to change.

It is a great tribute to Trotsky that, even when expelled from the Communist Party and exiled from Russia, he kept organising and never capitulated either to Stalin or to despair. It is that fight in the most difficult of circumstances that kept the genuine revolutionary socialist tradition alive for today. A tradition that stands for real equality, liberation and internationalism.

Trotsky's ideas, like Marx's before him, are not a dogma. He was not always right. Shortly before he was murdered, he predicted that both Western capitalism and Stalinism would be thrown into a deep crisis by the Second World War. He was eventually proved wrong on both counts, disorientating many of his followers after the war. It was left to future generations to build on and develop his ideas. But if some people have been able to see further, it is only because they stand on the shoulders of a giant. Trotsky's ideas and methods are full of lessons for a new generation resisting war and capitalism. For us, as for him, they are tools for changing the world and fighting for the future.

A GUIDE TO FURTHER READING

Trotsky was a powerful writer and his work is enormously rewarding to read. Both his autobiography *My Life* (Well Red, London, 2004) and above all his massive *History of the Russian Revolution* (Pluto, London, 2004) are literary masterpieces, and the latter is a brilliant defence of the revolution. His two classic statements of his theory of permanent revolution, *The Permanent Revolution* and *Results and Prospects*, are helpfully published together (Well Red, London, 2004). For the united front see the collections *The First Five Years of the Communist International* (in 2 volumes; New Park, London, 1973-4) and *The Struggle against Fascism in Germany* (Pathfinder, London and New York, 2001). The Marxist Internet Archive (www.marxists.org.uk) has an extensive collection of Trotsky's writings online.

Isaac Deutscher's trilogy *Trotsky: The Prophet Armed, The Prophet Unarmed* and *The Prophet Outcast* (all Verso, London 2003) is an outstanding work of biography, if sometimes flawed by the author's own politics. Tony Cliff's four-volume biography of Trotsky (published by Bookmarks) has a surer political grasp but is currently out of print. Duncan Hallas's *Trotsky's Marxism* (Bookmarks, London, 1987) is an excellent short discussion of Trotsky's ideas.

Trotsky's ideas have been developed further by a later generation of socialists. Tony Cliff's *Trotskyism After Trotsky* (Bookmarks, London, 1999) is a short guide to some key areas in which he and others built on Trotsky's ideas in the light of events after the Second World War. Cliff's *State Capitalism in Russia* (available at http://www.marxists.org.uk/archive/cliff/index) is a more detailed and pathbreaking analysis of Stalin's Russia that argues that it was a state capitalist regime.